A Picture Book of
John F. Kennedy

For Etan and Adina
D.A.A.

Text copyright © 1991 by David A. Adler
illustrations copyright © 1991 by Robert Casilla

Library of Congress Cataloging-in-Publication Data
Adler, David A.
A picture book of John F. Kennedy / by David A. Adler:
illustrated by Robert Casilla. —1st ed.
p. cm.
Summary: Depicts the life and career of John F. Kennedy.
ISBN 0-8234-0884-1
1. Kennedy, John F. (John Fitzgerald), 1917–1963—Juvenile
literature. 2. Presidents—United States—Biography—Juvenile
literature. [1. Kennedy, John F. (John Fitzgerald), 1917–1963.
2. Presidents.] I. Casilla, Robert, ill. II. Title.
E842.Z9A35 1991
973.922'092—dc20 90-23589 CIP AC
[B]
ISBN 0-8234-0884-1
ISBN 0-8234-0976-7 (pbk.)

A Picture Book of
John F. Kennedy

by David A. Adler

illustrated by Robert Casilla

Holiday House / New York

John F. Kennedy, the thirty-fifth president of the United States, was born on May 29, 1917, in Brookline, Massachusetts. His mother, Rose, was the daughter of the mayor of Boston. His father, Joseph, was a tough, rich businessman.

Joseph Kennedy raised his nine children to play hard and to play to win. He was determined that one of them would be president of the United States.

John was the second of the Kennedy children. As a child he was nicknamed "Jack." Later he would be called by his initials, JFK.

Joseph and Rose Kennedy with their eight children in 1931. Jack is second from the left. Edward would be born the following year.

Young Jack Kennedy was thin and often sick. He had scarlet fever, whooping cough, jaundice, hepatitis, back trouble, and other ailments—But when he played sports, he played hard. He played against bigger and stronger boys, and he played to win.

Jack is farthest to right.

Jack went to private schools. He wasn't a very good student, but he had lots of friends. In high school he and his friends got into plenty of mischief. The school's head-master called the boys "bad apples," but still, he was charmed by young Jack Kennedy's smile.

In 1936 Jack entered Harvard. By his third year, he became serious about his studies. He graduated with honors in 1940.

While Jack was in college, there was trouble in Europe.

On September 1, 1939, the German army invaded Poland. Two days later France and England declared war on Germany. The Second World War had begun.

Jack's father was the United States ambassador to England. Jack visited his father in England and he traveled to other countries in Europe. When he returned to Harvard, he wrote a paper on why England was not ready for the war with Germany. His paper was later published as a book, *Why England Slept*. It became a best-seller.

Jack's older brother, Joe Jr., was a Navy flyer during the war. He was on a dangerous mission when his plane exploded, and he was killed. Now Joseph Kennedy's dream, that one of his children would become president, was centered on Jack.

(FROM LEFT TO RIGHT) *Jack Kennedy, his father Joseph Kennedy, and his brother Joe Kennedy, Jr.*

On September 1, 1939, the German army invaded Poland. Two days later France and England declared war on Germany. The Second World War had begun.

Jack's father was the United States ambassador to England. Jack visited his father in England and he traveled to other countries in Europe. When he returned to Harvard, he wrote a paper on why England was not ready for the war with Germany. His paper was later published as a book, *Why England Slept*. It became a best-seller.

In September 1941 Jack enlisted in the United States Navy. Less than three months later, early on the morning of December 7, 1941, United States' ships, planes, and soldiers were attacked by Japanese bombers at Pearl Harbor, Hawaii. The United States was at war.

Jack commanded a small navy boat, PT 109. In August 1943, while at sea, his boat was cut in half by a passing Japanese destroyer. Jack held on to an injured crew member and swam for five hours until they reached shore. Jack was given a Navy medal for his bravery.

Jack's older brother, Joe Jr., was a Navy flyer during the war. He was on a dangerous mission when his plane exploded, and he was killed. Now Joseph Kennedy's dream, that one of his children would become president, was centered on Jack.

(FROM LEFT TO RIGHT) *Jack Kennedy, his father Joseph Kennedy, and his brother Joe Kennedy, Jr.*

In 1946 Jack ran for a seat in the United States House of Representatives. His whole family helped out. He won the election easily. He was re-elected in 1948 and again in 1950.

In 1952 Jack ran for the United States Senate. The family helped again. Jack's father gave money to the campaign. His mother invited women to tea and told them about Jack. His brother Robert managed the campaign. Jack Kennedy won in a close election.

Jack after his election in 1946 with his parents and grandparents.

Senator John F. Kennedy was a war hero and a best-selling author. He was young, rich, and handsome. Women visited the senate just to watch him.

In 1951 Jack met Jacqueline "Jackie" Bouvier, a pretty, smart young woman from a wealthy family. She worked for a newspaper. They dated, and while she was working in England, he sent a telegraph to her. It said, "You are missed." When Jackie returned, she and Jack became engaged. They married on September 12, 1953.

In the fall of 1954, Jack had an operation on his back. While he was in the hospital, he wrote a second book, *Profiles in Courage*. It was awarded the 1957 Pulitzer Prize for biography.

Jack Kennedy was re-elected to the senate in 1956. Then on January 2, 1960, he announced that he hoped to be the Democratic party's nominee for President. Seven months later, after a hard campaign, he won the nomination.

The Republican party nominated Vice President Richard M. Nixon. Kennedy and Nixon met in four television debates. Kennedy seemed more relaxed than Nixon during the debates and better prepared, too.

On November 8, 1960, in a close vote, Jack Kennedy was elected president of the United States.

John F. Kennedy was the youngest man and the first Roman Catholic ever elected president. He was sworn in on January 20, 1961. He said in his speech, "And so my fellow Americans, ask not what your country can do for you—ask what you can do for your country. My fellow citizens of the world, ask not what America will do for you, but what together we can do for the freedom of man."

Americans were excited to have a young man and his family in the White House. President Kennedy's daughter, Caroline, rode her pet horse on the White House lawn. His son, John Jr., played under his desk. Women watched how his wife, Jackie, dressed, and copied her.

Jack Kennedy supported the rights of black people. He set up the Peace Corps. It sent American volunteers to help poor countries in Africa, Asia, and Latin America. He supported the arts and a strong space program.

In October 1962 President Kennedy learned that the Russians had sent weapons to nearby Cuba—missiles that could hit the United States in minutes. Kennedy ordered navy ships to surround the island of Cuba and keep out any more weapons. A few days later, the Russians removed the missiles.

President Kennedy and Soviet Premier Khrushchev signed a treaty limiting the testing of nuclear weapons.

On November 22, 1963, President Kennedy and Jacqueline were in Dallas, Texas. They rode in an open car, waving to huge crowds of people. Suddenly there were three rifle shots. The president fell forward. He had been killed.

Radio and television programs were interrupted with the tragic news. The American people were shocked and horrified.

Lee Harvey Oswald was accused of killing the president. He was arrested. Two days later he, too, was killed. He was shot by Jack Ruby.

President John F. Kennedy was a hero to millions of people. He was one of America's most loved presidents. He reduced the chances of nuclear war, he brought help and hope to our nation's minorities, and to the poor, sick, and aged. When President John F. Kennedy died, the country mourned his death. Some of the hope and promise that Americans had for a brighter future seemed to die with him.

IMPORTANT DATES

1917	Born on May 29 in Brookline, Massachusetts.
1940	Graduated from Harvard.
1941–1945	Served in the United States Navy during the Second World War.
1946–1953	Served in the United States Congress.
1953	Married Jacqueline Bouvier on September 12.
1953–1961	Served in the United States Senate.
1960	Announced on January 2 that he was a candidate for president.
1960	Elected President of the United States on November 8.
1963	Assassinated on November 22.

John Jr. at his father's funeral.